How

your LIFE in the

next 15 minutes

RAHUL BADAMI

CONTENTS

INTRODUCTION:
SELF-BELIEF ALLOWS YOU TO PREDICT THE FUTURE

When I first thought of writing a book on Self Belief my inner self asked me, "Are you the right person to talk about Self Belief?"

I thought about it. I am just an ordinary person. I have had many situations in my life where I questioned my abilities, and whether I was doing the right thing. My belief in myself cannot be called perfect. I am not there yet. So why will anyone read my book?

Then I decided it doesn't matter if no one reads my book. I will write this book for my own self. To inspire myself. To tell myself what I need to do to steel my belief. And if others read it, I would be happy when they find value in my strategies to change their lives.

I didn't question myself any further and started to take action on writing this book. And this is what self belief is actually about. Using right thoughts and productive actions to predict the future.

If I see myself completing this book, and then going back to this chapter to re-read it, it will tell me that my vision of publishing this book is manifested.

How can you change your life?

It all starts with belief. Belief is an intangible emotion that determines the course of everyone's life. The only way to measure belief is by evaluating the quality of your life. If you want to improve the quality of your life, you have to increase your self belief.

My experience has shown me that the only way we change our belief is through our thoughts and actions.

The relation between Thoughts, Actions and Self Belief can be expressed in two statements. One statement will keep you where you are. The other will unleash the power inside of you.

The first statement is: **Our beliefs direct our thoughts and actions.**

Would you agree that it's true?

Consider a boy thinking of asking a girl out for prom. What if he believes she wouldn't be interested in him, and would get bored of his company? The boy would not take the action of asking her out. And because the action wasn't taken, the belief would be reinforced. And the cycle will continue.

LESS BELIEF > LIMITING THOUGHTS > MINIMAL OR NO ACTION > LESS BELIEF

Is there a way out? Yes, of course.

Surprisingly, the reverse holds true as well. **Our thoughts and actions direct our belief.**

EMPOWERING THOUGHTS > MASSIVE ACTION > STRONGER BELIEF > EMPOWERING THOUGHTS

The first statement doesn't give us much control over our beliefs. But we can use the second statement to change our beliefs and get what we want. The biggest secret of successful people is that even if they don't know everything, they still charge ahead towards their goals.

You don't have to get it right; you just have to get started.

So let's get started. I have purposefully kept this book short and to the point. Your time is important. I don't want to overwhelm you with a dozen strategies over hundreds of pages. Nor do I want to beat around the bush with ineffective filler type paragraphs, when effective & succinct information can be provided in a few concise words.

While we are on the topic of conciseness, this book can be described in just one sentence: How to use productive thoughts and productive actions, to strengthen our belief system?

To answer that question, this book is divided into two sections. The first section talks about how our thoughts shape our belief, and how we can use the right thoughts to build a productive belief system. The second section is about taking action towards our dreams, and using those actions to strengthen our beliefs about our dreams.

(Side Note: As you can see from the second statement, Empowering Thoughts initiate the process of increasing your self-belief. I have found that listening to Affirmations is a simple yet powerful way to empower your thoughts. After searching (in vain) for an Affirmations audio that could be a good complement to this book, I decided to create one myself. You can download the Affirmations MP3 for free at http://FreePositiveAffirmations.com)

SECTION ONE:
THOUGHTS THAT'S STRENGHTEN BELIEF

1
WE THINK ONLY TWICE IN A YEAR

"Few people think more than two or three times a year. I have made an international reputation for myself by thinking once or twice a week."

Do you know who spoke these interesting words?

It was George Bernard Shaw. Had he gone bonkers when he disclosed his thinking habits? Is it really possible that one of the greatest thinkers of yesteryears thought only once a week? From my personal experience I would say yes.

Preposterous?

Not so. Mr. Shaw is actually right.

There was a time some years back when I used to consider myself a thinker. I used to spend significant amounts of time dwelling on my life and my future. Today I realize that what I was actually doing was replaying a couple of original thoughts again and again. It couldn't be called sustained creative thinking.

In fact we rarely think. Whatever thought processes that happen in our minds on a daily basis are simply repeated commands. Our routine habits are so entrenched that we barely register brushing our teeth, eating or even driving our car.

Would you think the work you do at your job or business requires you to think? The surprising answer is no.

Even though your work requires complex thought process, once you have been in the same role for more than 3 months, the decision making is repetitive rather than creative. The only time people think at work is during the first few days of a new job, or if there have been an unprecedented turn of events that force you to change your normal work habits.

So what has your thinking got to do with belief? First, our beliefs are the reason we are at our current place in the journey of life. Positive beliefs, positive journey. Negative or neutral beliefs, mediocre journey.

How do we get back in the habit of sustained creative thinking? It can be done by making a conscious effort to allocate 15-30 minutes daily to ask profoundly thoughtful questions of ourselves. This can be done either the first thing in the day or the last one at night. For now, don't worry about the questions that you should ask yourself. I will provide a list of questions in a later chapter to jumpstart your creativity.

2

THINKING IS PRAYING

I am an agnostic. While I don't believe in everything that religion tells us about God, I believe that there is a Power that permeates through the universe. This Universal Power works within us, and through us. We can make this Universal Power our closest friend and ally.

The ancients used to tell us the power of prayer. Unfortunately, the true meaning of prayer has been lost in translation over the centuries.

Until now.

Most people don't realize that every moment in their life, they are praying. And the Universal Power is giving them exactly what they are praying for.

How is that possible?

It is through the power of thoughts. When you are thinking, you are praying. Your thoughts, whether conscious or unconscious, will be received as a prayer to the Universal Power, who will make it work exactly like you wish for. Your quality of life is in direct proportion to the quality of your thoughts.

But, wait a minute. You didn't pray for a lousy job, a crushing debt, or lukewarm relations with your friends and family. I am here to tell you that is exactly what you prayed for. I will further rub it in and say that your thoughts have brought you to your current station in life.

Does that thought make you uncomfortable?

Well, congratulations! You succeeded in thinking outside your comfort zone. Being uncomfortable is a great sign. Because it means that you are learning something new.

Here are some famous quotes to ponder:

A man is what he thinks about all day long - Ralph Waldo Emerson.

As a man thinketh in his heart, so is he - The Bible.

You become what you think about - Earl Nightingale called his aphorism 'the strangest secret'.

All three quotes solely and unequivocally put the onus on ourselves and our thoughts, for who we become. The good news is that it means that our life can be drastically altered by changing the pattern of our thoughts.

Now that you understand the power of prayer and its relationship with thoughts, it's time to take your awareness to the next level. You will be able to realize why things have worked, or not worked in your life. Consider this.

If thoughts are prayer, then our God is only as strong as our thoughts.

If your dreams are not in alignment with your life, and what you do on a day to day basis, it means that your thoughts aren't strong enough to move you to where you want to be. You may be unconsciously bounding your potential. Your inner voice may be telling you that 'this is the best you can do' or 'you are not capable of doing xyz'.

Most people don't realize that they have an inner critic that thwarts them at every turn and kills their success. This inner critic has been inside of you since your childhood. It has been strengthened each time you heard 'No'.

Shad Helmsletter, author of 'What to say, when you talk to yourself' revealed in his book that the typical child hears

'No' around 150,000 times by the age of 18. That is a shocking statistic of how we are conditioned even before we can think rationally for ourselves.

The best way to identify if you have an inner critic is to observe your actions.

Are you procrastinating on your goals?

Bingo! Your inner critic has chained you down with a 'cant-do' message. The best method I have found to get over this 'No' conditioning is through the power of affirmations.

Affirmations basically mean that you talk to yourself about yourself in a positive manner. This de-stresses you and makes you more relaxed and confident. I have been listening to affirmations daily for a couple of years and it has literally transformed how I think about myself and my capabilities.

You can download my own Affirmations audio MP3 absolutely free at http://freepositiveaffirmations.com . Make sure that you are listening to it daily, so that over a period of time the positive vibes from the affirmations sink into your subconscious. The best time I have discovered to listen to the affirmations is when you are in the bathtub. That is the time when you have the least distractions.

3

ASKING HARD QUESTIONS

One of my friends loves food. Naturally he has belly fat. If I have to tell him to lose his belly fat, what advice do you think I should give him?

How about if I were to tell him, "Eat less and exercise more." Would that be a good suggestion? Yes, I think that would be a very good suggestion. It would be the best way for him to be lean and slim.

But there's a catch.

Even I have belly fat.

So before I suggest anything to him, I should be following my own advice.

Too many times, we have all the answers to life's major questions like how to lose weight, how to spend less and save more, how to have better relationships, how to do a better job. But we don't implement them even if they are straight forward common sense.

Why?

Because the answers are not the issue here, it's the questions we ask of ourselves.

The hardest question isn't beating yourself up by asking, "Why didn't I take action towards my goals?" It is by asking,

"Why should I take action towards this goal?" Or at an even more primary level, "Is this, the right goal for me?"

We usually equate hard questions as questions that will make us squirm and bring on feelings of futility. No. Hard questions are those that take us right back to the start and even question whether you are on the right path.

Here's a profound thought that has guided me to improve the quality of my life: *Life is not about getting the right answers. It's about asking the right questions of ourselves.*

The better the questions we ask, the better we are able to guide ourselves.

Create a framework of tough questions that you ask yourself every day. This will help spur your creativity and keep you set on your track. Take a printout of these questions and paste them on a wall or somewhere where you can see it every day.

The most fundamental question we need to ask ourselves is:

What is my purpose in life?

My easiest and simplest definition of 'purpose' is, *doing something worthwhile that gives you lasting happiness.*

Some simple things can make you temporarily happy, but they cannot be your purpose for living. You will be happy after gorging down on a McFlurry. The question to ask is, did you do something worthwhile and whether it will give you lasting happiness.

Discovering your purpose is the first step towards a fulfilling life. Remember that *we discover our purpose through trial and error.*

What comes naturally to me? What am I inherently better at?

Knowing what you are good at could be a good indicator of where your purpose should lie. Are you finding it difficult to evaluate what you are good at? That's natural. We tend to underestimate things we are good at and try to downplay it.

"Oh, anyone can cook."

"Anyone can be observant."

"Everyone can raise good children."

"Everyone can maintain a good relation with their spouse."

But the reality is not everyone can do what you can easily do. You will have to search hard to find what you excel at. Remember that *your purpose should be in alignment to your temperament.*

If I did everyday what I did today for the next few years, would I be closer to my purpose and happiness?

Answer in a simple yes or no.

This question is actually a checkpoint that will gauge whether you are on the right path. It evaluates whether your daily habits are in line with your purpose. If your answer for today is No, ask yourself if you worked on something in the past week or month towards your purpose. Was there any recent activity you did that would put you on the path of lasting happiness?

If the answer to this question is also No, I would strongly suggest you to take a hard look at how your life is set up, and evaluate what you will need to do to align yourself with your purpose.

SECTION TWO:
ACTIONS THAT STRENGTHEN BELIEF

1

WHY 'THE LAW OF ATTRACTION' WILL NEVER WORK?

When I first watched the movie 'The Secret', I was absolutely thrilled by it. It was like THE answer to my prayers. I could now simply think the right thoughts to attract health, wealth, and happiness in my life. I may have viewed the movie dozens of times to understand the secret, and how I could use it.

But try as much as I could to think positive thoughts, and wait for the universe to align with my thoughts, nothing happened. My dreams were just that. Dreams.

Eventually, I got disillusioned and stopped believing in the Law of Attraction. And I am not the only one. There are millions who have shared a similar experience.

Why the Law of Attraction that worked for thousands of people, didn't work for millions?

Here's the answer.

Like others, I was expecting the Law of Attraction to give me something for almost nothing. I just had to sit back and dream and the Universe would provide me with everything. I had fallen into the common misconception of taking the Law of Attraction literally. There is a crucial concept that hasn't been drilled down in the movie 'The Secret' which has led to the ineffectiveness in the Law of Attraction.

The Law is not about Attraction, it's about ~~ATTR~~ ACTION.

Or in other words, its actual name should have been 'The Law of Action'. Also known as the Law of Cause and Effect, this is the real driving force behind the entire Universe. I would like to call this as the real Universal Power.

Action is the only thing that can shake up things, prevent you from stagnating, bring beneficial changes, and greatly improve your life situation. Action is the only method through which you can align your body (doer) with your mind (thinker) to realize your dreams (future). Unfortunately, sitting and wishing has never helped anyone, nor will it ever work for anyone, especially you.

Feels hard to accept this?

It was very tough for me to digest this fact. I was stubborn enough to think that things will automatically go the way I wanted. Years passed, and I was still stuck in the same place. I passed my entire twenties (a decade if you will) and went almost into my mid-thirties before I realized this. (I admit I am a slow learner.)

What is your own age? Would you find it hard to believe that a dozen years would just pass by, and you will find out that you still haven't worked on your major life goals? Trust me, it will happen without action.

To put it in the simplest words. No Cause. No Effect.

On the other hand. Do Cause. Get Effects.

Now even if you know that you have to take action, your belief system stops you, because it knows that you are wandering into unchartered territory. Your belief system wants to drag you back into its comfort zone.

This is why doing something new is so tough. Your brain has been wired to keep you in the same stagnant place. And it will deliver thoughts to you that will question why you are going on this unknown new path.

"This will never work."

"Why are you attempting this?"

"This will require lot of money upfront."

"No one in our family has done this."

"Am I doing the right thing?"

These thoughts will freeze you from taking action.

In the introductory section, I mentioned that instead of getting it right, it's more important that you get started. Prima facie, it may seem illogical, but my experience and the experience of successful people have validated this concept.

A study was made some years back wherein students were divided into two groups. One group was told to create a single project report but it had to be perfect. The other group had to create five project reports in the same time-frame, but the quality was allowed to be average.

Any guesses which group ended with the better quality?

It was the second group who were allowed to dish out an average quality report.

And what happened to the first group?

They got so involved in polishing their work. Making endless improvements that at the end, no report got submitted.

The second group's goal was focused on quantity. They won because they had to get out five reports through the door. The first group was focused on quality and their inner critic was so tough on them that they simply froze and didn't take action to submit the report for fear of being ridiculed.

So take action first. Average people who are action-takers are more successful then geniuses who want to roll out the perfect invention.

Look at Microsoft or any other software vendor. The first release of a product has so many bugs, that within days they roll out a patch to fix it. And as you know Microsoft has been the most famous software vendor of the past decade. They were successful because they understand that it's better to get the product out of the door, than spend months wondering what bugs they missed. Their customers will anyhow tell them what's wrong, and they go back and fix it.

As mentioned earlier... do cause, get effects. Take action now.

2

TAKING TOUGH ACTIONS THROUGH SINGLE-TASKING

Whose dream are you living?

I am asking this question because taking action is easy when you are doing something that you inherently love.

If I look at my own life, for the first couple of decades I was living out my parent's dreams to see me graduate and be successful at a job. The next decade was spent in living my manager's dream of being the ideal employee. Only now I have started to break away and started doing something that I love. So I ask again.

Whose dream is it anyway? Yours? Your parents? Spouse? Peers? Kids?

My dream is to provide value to others through my writings. I have a dream of reading a billion words and writing a million. And to do that I will have to buckle down and spend consistent time everyday to both read and write. For me the tough action is neither reading or writing; it's the discipline to do the reading and writing *on a daily basis without fail.*

I floundered for months writing my first book. After eighteen months, I had only completed half of it. However, once I had disciplined myself through a daily ritual, I was able to complete the remainder of my book in just one month.

So what is your dream? Are you taking daily action towards it? Are your actions consistent? If not, why?

My personal experience has shown me that I don't take action when I am distracted. The average person has multiple responsibilities and tasks that distract them away from whatever they want. But I found one very simple technique to overcome my procrastination and stay focused.

I call it Single-Tasking.

Time-management gurus have been harping for decades about multi-tasking. Multi-tasking means being able to do multiple things simultaneously. However, recent studies in brain science have painted a completely different picture. Multi-tasking only works for subconscious or deeply-embedded habits like driving a car.

You cannot *consciously* multi-task.

In other words, you cannot do two things that require your complete attention at the same time. You cannot solve a crossword puzzle and create a grocery list at the same time. Your mind gets stressed out, and it reacts by going back into its comfort zone of subconscious habits. These habits then keep you where you are.

Give yourself a break. Make it easy for your brain to help you out. This can happen by gently nudging your mind towards just ONE activity.

Here's what I do: I don't keep a big list of things that I have to do daily. I take up only one major thing that I have to accomplish that day. The secret is that I stick to that activity till it's completed. It may take one day. It may take a week. But the important thing is that I make more progress than when my mind is burdened with multiple tasks.

(Sidenote: To clarify, single-tasking means I allocate a significant chunk of the workday towards my major task. I do other things only if they cannot be avoided. Make sure that you do your major task in a continuous uninterrupted span of time. Other things can and should wait.)

If you still aren't convinced of the power of single-tasking, and are worried about the other tasks piling up, paint the following picture in your mind.

Visualize a car with four steering wheels for all four passengers. However, all four passengers want to go in different directions and each of them tries to turn their steering wheel in their direction and then screams at the other three for not cooperating. The car will twist and turn, but go nowhere.

Your mind is the car, and the passengers are the tasks. And this is what happens inside your mind when you multi-task.

On the other hand, when you are single-tasking, it's just one person steering the car, while the other three quietly wait their turn at driving. The experience is much smoother, and less stressful.

So if you are worried about other activities that are pending, remind yourself that you are already progressing well towards one task. And when that task is finished, not only will you be very happy, but also your mind will be free to concentrate on the next task.

However, some tasks don't come naturally to us. In some cases, we try but somehow we find it very hard even if we are completely focused on it.

It is because of what I call situational self-belief. There are some things that we can easily do, and other things that we struggle with. It is not as if the things that we can easily do are by default easy. It's just that we have more confidence and assurance when performing that work.

But, if that task is important to your future, you will have to do it. You cannot avoid it.

Successful people make a habit of doing things they don't like to do. If you are an entrepreneur, you may not like calling prospects. If you are in a job, you may feel inhibited when doing something outside of your job role. The thing is - you have to take action. Nothing in this world can replace good old-fashioned action. And this is what all successful people know. And they have done it again and again. They have faced uncertainty, fear and apprehension. Today they are used to it.

Being successful is simply a set of right actions that few people do. Its time you did it. Start today.

The next chapter will tell you why.

3

WHY ITS CRITICAL TO SUCCEED JUST TODAY

Most goal-setters and goal-setting exercises simply get it wrong.

Our brain simply cannot picture a long-term goal; say what you will be five years from now. I don't know about you, but personally my mind gets real fuzzy around the details. Short term goals have an urgency and clarity to them that beat any long-term goals hands down.

Forget yearly resolutions. Monthly goals are the best. I would recommend that you start with a specific goal that you want to do this month.

Let's say you want to contact a hundred prospects for your business in a month. That would mean at least three every day. So focus only on today. Contact those three prospects. Don't fret over yesterday. Don't worry about tomorrow. Simply focus on being successful *today*. In this case success means completing your daily actions.

A successful future implies successful years. A successful year implies successful months, successful weeks, and at its most fundamental unit, a successful day.

Today is where you should be focused on. Just ensure that you get through today with your actions.

The most profound thing I have experienced is that consistency leads to success. You don't need to look beyond top athletes to understand what I am talking about. They work towards their dreams every day.

Every day.

That's the key.

Listen up. This is one of the most profound things I have learned, and then experienced.

What you do today can change your life.

Your life will NOT change one fine day in the future. It can change only TODAY.

When I was a teenager, I had painted a rosy picture of one fine day in the future where everything would be like a wonderland a decade later. The ten years came and went by and nothing changed in the slightest.

Why?

It was because I was always imagining a day in the future. It had no links to what I was doing today. If you picture yourself doing something different tomorrow, are you doing some part of that activity today? If not, you are in *disconnect* from your ideal future.

In my case, my daily habits stayed as they are, and they kept me where I was. To rephrase, my habits (daily actions) kept me in TODAY, and my thoughts kept me in TOMORROW.

Don't be the delusional fool that I was. Your thoughts and actions should both be in TODAY. The only way to succeed tomorrow is to succeed today. And the only way to succeed today is to change what you are doing this minute. Change this minute, and your life changes... eventually.

The promise of your life's eventual change is something that's hard to swallow. We want everything to change instantly. However, any change that we do today, will take some time to garner results. But knowing that you have to change this minute still doesn't give the complete picture.

The true secret is *change* and *consistency*.

It makes no sense in changing your habits today, and when the next day comes, you are back to your old habits. The key is being consistent at it for days, months and years. You will have to string hundreds of successful TODAYs, before your TOMORROW changes. Even if there are days when you don't get to work towards your purpose, put it behind you and move on. Get cracking on the next day.

I recently completed a book on the corporate workplace. For me to complete it, I had to write consistently every day. I was able to write a minimum of couple hundred words every day and was able to finish it in a little over a month.

Now consider the performance of this book. Unfortunately, there were hardly a few days in a row that I was able to write. The daily word count was way less, and overall my writing was inconsistent with days of no writings. It took me nearly three months to finish this book.

But this book is completed. So is it a success or failure?

Here's how I define success: Attainment of one's goal by focusing back on it even after getting sidetracked multiple times.

I have a day job, a wife & kid, and multiple other responsibilities. But what separates a success from failure is how you get back on track towards your goal each time you are distracted.

As Paulo Coelho talks about in the introductory section of his wonderful book 'The Alchemist', "*The secret of life is to fall seven times and get up eight times.*" Every time you fall (fail at your goals, miss opportunities, something comes up) don't get emotional about it. You haven't missed your goals in the big scheme of life. You have just been delayed. Keep doing your Daily Actions unemotionally, and it will take you closer to your dreams.

Before you embark on the final section, make sure you have twenty minutes to spare. This is very important. Five minutes to read the section and fifteen minutes to take the action steps that I will note. As discussed in this chapter, changing what you do moment to moment, changes your life.

BONUS SECTION

1

HOW DO I USE THIS INFORMATION TO CHANGE MY LIFE IN THE NEXT FIFTEEN MINUTES

Things you will need:

A good old Letter/A4 sized paper

A pen (a computer & printer can be used, but is not necessary)

Common Sense

Patience (You are doing something new. Don't be hard on yourself)

Note: Once your goal is completed, come back to this book and repeat the below process again. I have boiled down the 'change your life' process to 5 simple but powerful steps. They are purposely kept simple so that they will be easy to follow. Don't for a moment underestimate the simplicity of the 5 steps below. They are designed to get you in action mode immediately. And most importantly, consistency is the key. You will have to stick at this every day till it's complete.

The good news is that the more you follow this process, the easier it will become eventually.

Step 1: Write down three things that you want to accomplish this year.

Step 2: Sort them in the order of priority with the most important (to you) at number 1 position.

Step 3: Scratch out number 2 and 3. This way you will be focused on only one Task.

Step 4: Now write out your goal as follows: "I will complete [Task] by the 30th of this month. (It doesn't matter which date of the month you are reading this. The lesser the number of days, the more focused your mind will be.)

Step 5: Close this book and start NOW.

2

EXCERPT FROM MY BOOK
I AM GOD: WORLD'S OLDEST STORY

This book uses the medium of fiction to explain the concept of self-belief. A prehistoric tale that will take you on a journey of discovering the divinity that has always been hidden within you waiting to be unleashed. Here's what a few readers had to say:

"A powerful story... Absolutely loved the book!"

"Highly recommended for anyone looking to be uplifted and inspired!"

* * * * *

150,000 years ago. Near the Awash River, Africa.

Ayot reached Frew's hut and as was the norm knocked the side with a rock. Frew's voice bade him to enter. Frew was looking better than yesterday. He was up and about, brandishing his favorite weapon; a long piece of wood with blunt ends that he used as a cudgel.

"Ayot, my boy. It's so good that you came up to meet me. How are the Tasks going on?"

"Not so well, Frew. I haven't made any progress yet."

"That's alright. We still have many days before the full moon blooms. I have faith in you. I am sure that you will fulfill your destiny."

Ayot felt a bit embarrassed by the faith put in him by the oldest and most experienced member of the tribe. He looked at Frew; at the dark eyes that had seen a lot through many years. And yet, Frew had felt that Ayot was the most deserving candidate to succeed their Chief. "You have so much belief in me. Why cannot I have the same belief in myself?"

Frew looked at him for a moment. "Have you ever looked upon your reflection in a pond? How the still water shows the features on your face?"

"Countless times. Why?"

"Have you ever noticed it shows you only one side of your face?"

Ayot thought about that. He had never observed that he had been looking at only one angle of his face, one aspect of his image.

Frew continued. "Precisely in the same way when you think; you think only from one angle. Your beliefs, thoughts and actions are borne of your one-sided image. It may or may not be accurate. However, only an impartial observer can see you from all sides, not to mention understand you, taking into consideration all your aspects."

"Are you saying that I need to believe in your faith towards me? And that your faith will increase my belief?" Ayot was puzzled.

"No. You will have belief in yourself only when you are able to see all the aspects that make up your character. You will come to know your strengths and weaknesses and will be able to guide yourself better. And also be able to accurately predict the outcome of any event."

"So, self-belief allows you to predict your future?"

"In a way, yes."

* * * * *

Want to read more?
Go here:
http://www.amazon.com/dp/B00CLHISYK/

Made in the USA
Las Vegas, NV
11 May 2021